Shark Girl

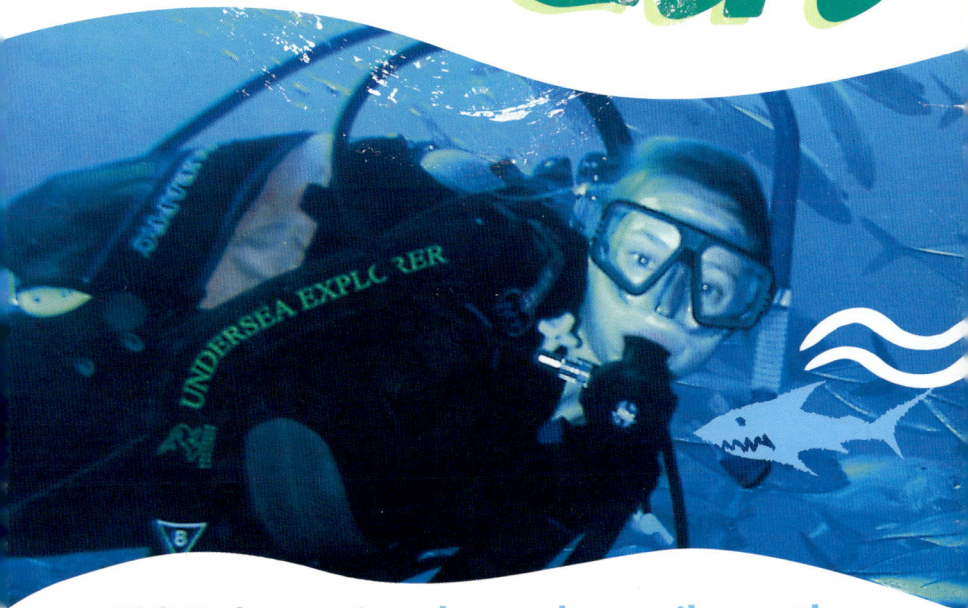

Nikki's home is a boat that sails on the Great Barrier Reef. She thinks it's the best place in the world for scuba divers to live — read on to find out why.

THOMSON

NELSON

Australia · Canada · Mexico · Singapore · Spain · United Kingdom · United States

THOMSON
NELSON

Zebras are published by Thomson Learning Australia
and are distributed as follows:

AUSTRALIA
Thomson Learning Australia
102 Dodds Street
Southbank 3006
Victoria

NEW ZEALAND
Nelson Price Milburn
1 Te Puni Street
Petone
Wellington

First published in 2002
10 9 8 7 6 5 4 3 2 1
05 04 03 02

Text © black dog books 2002
Shark Girl
ISBN 0 17010754 X
ISBN 0 17010846 5 Zebras Set B

a black dog (Australia) book

Designed by Watershed Design
Photographs and cover by Mark Norman
Photographs on p. iii, 1, 2, 5, 11, 15, 20 by David Paul
Photograph on p. 24 by Roger Fenwick
Illustration on p. iv by Guy Holt Design

Teacher consultant: Garry Chapman, Ivanhoe Grammar School

Printed in China by Midas Printing (Asia) Ltd

This title is published under the imprint of Nelson School.
Nelson Australia Pty Limited ACN 058 280 149
(incorporated in Victoria) trading as Thomson Learning Australia.

Distributed exclusively in the United Kingdom
and Ireland by:
Horwitz Gardner Limited
168e High Street
Egham
Surrey TW20 9HP
Customer Service Telephone 01784 477470

Contents

North America

South America

Europe

Africa

Asia

Australia

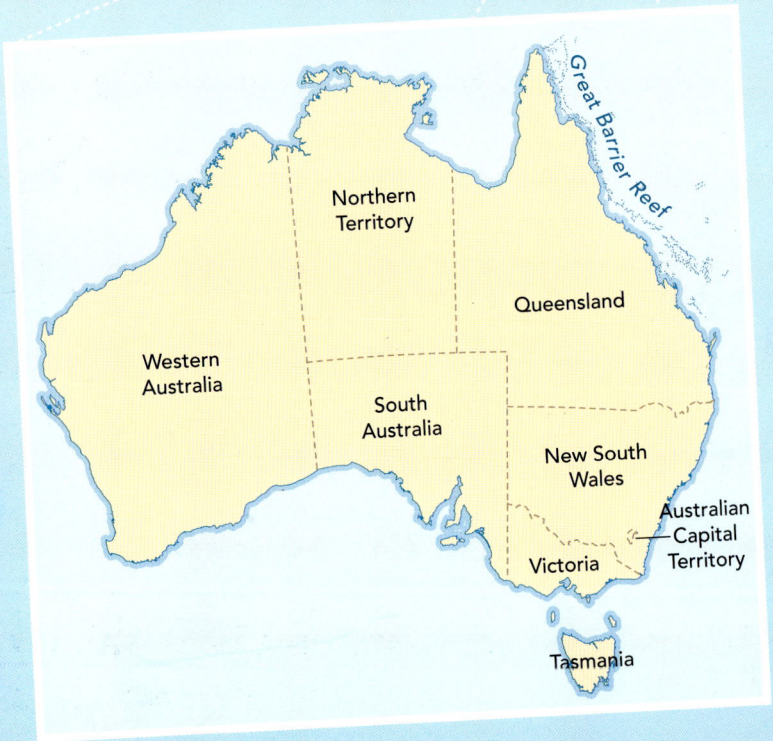

Great Barrier Reef

Northern
Territory

Queensland

Western
Australia

South
Australia

New South
Wales

Australian
Capital
Territory

Victoria

Tasmania

Chapter One

Going Diving

This is our boat, the **Undersea Explorer.**

Hi, I'm Nikki and I live on a boat with my dad. We take people on diving **expeditions** exploring the Great Barrier **Reef**.

1

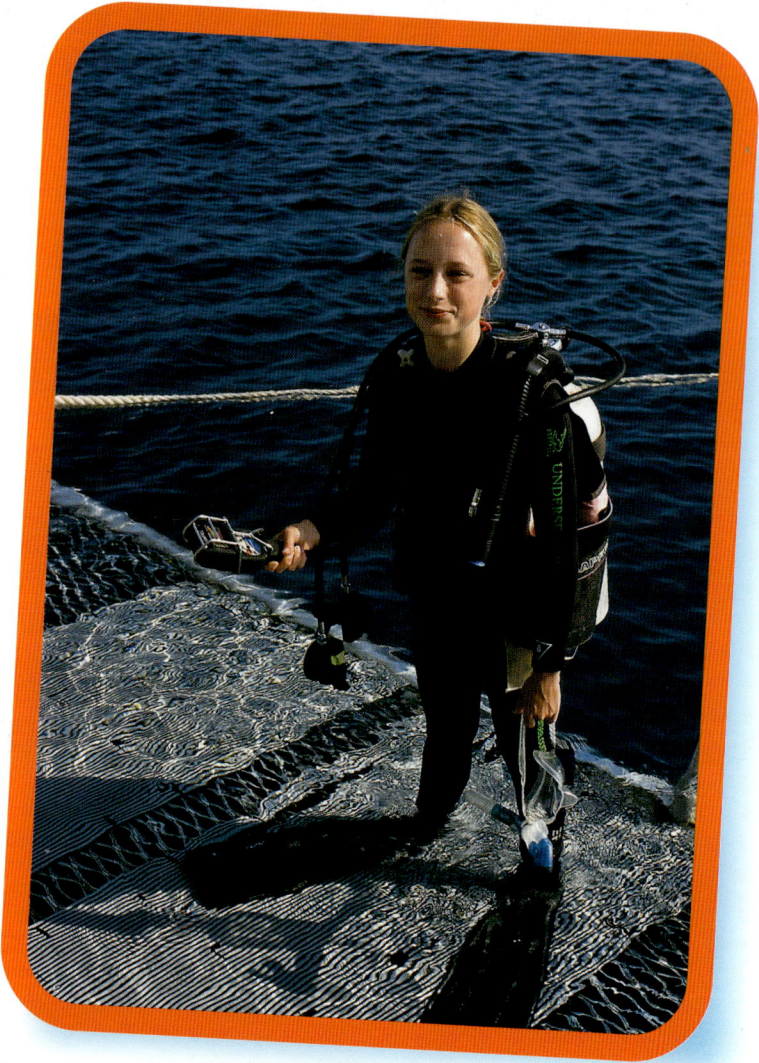

Here I am checking my dive gear before I go in the water.

I've been diving with my dad for a couple of years. I started just snorkelling, which means I swam mainly on the surface of the water. Then I moved on to **scuba** diving.

The letters in the word 'scuba' stand for self contained underwater breathing apparatus.

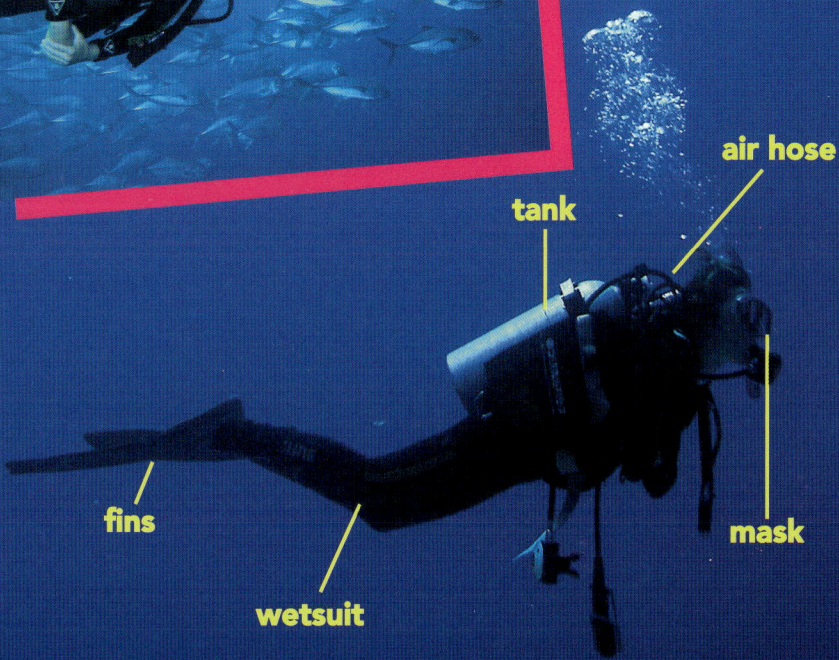

air hose

tank

fins

mask

wetsuit

To dive below the surface, I use scuba gear which lets me breathe under water.

The tank on my back is full of **compressed** air. There is an air hose that lets me breathe normally and my mask helps me see under water.

Scuba gear allows me to explore all sorts of places.

The Great Barrier Reef, where we dive, is 2,000 kilometres long. It is made up of thousands of coral reefs and hundreds of islands surrounded by warm blue water.

Chapter Two

Millions of Fish

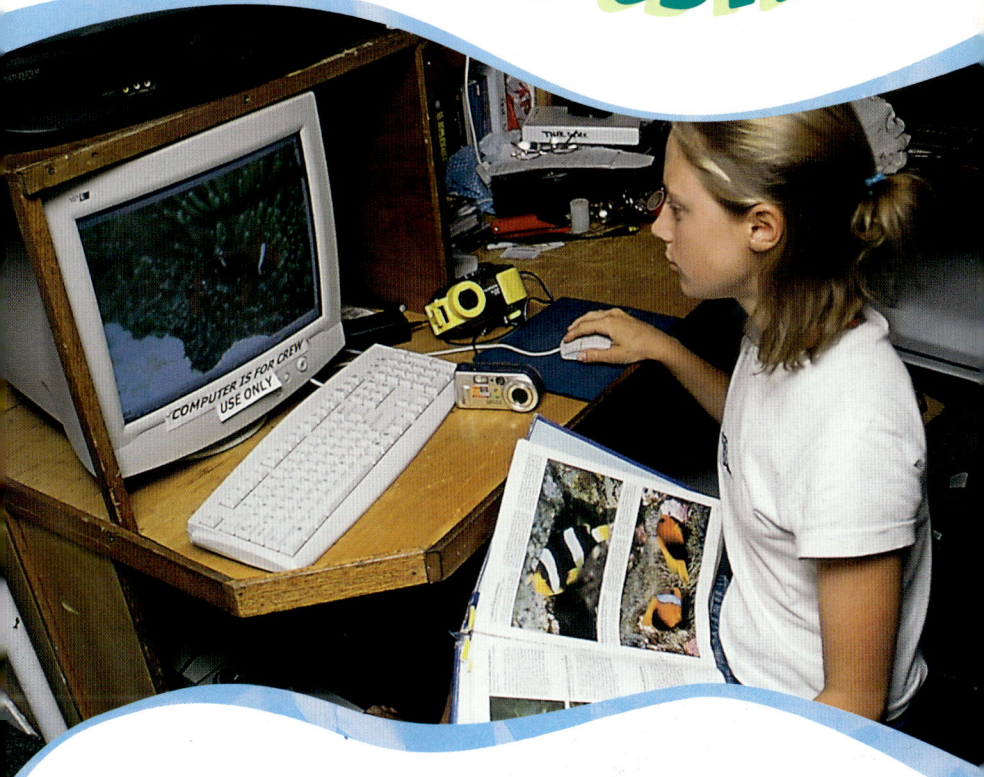

Since I started diving, I've become really interested in **marine** life. To find out about the things I see under water, I use books and the boat's computer.

Coral Cod

hawkfish

goatfish and sea perch

The Great Barrier Reef is home to millions of fish and other marine life. When divers visit this area, they can see some of the most spectacular underwater sights in the world.

Purple Anthias

I record these sights with a special digital camera that can be used under water. I take photographs of all the colourful and wonderful marine life that I see.

After my dive, I can look at the pictures on the onboard computer.

clownfish

One of my favourite groups of fish is the clownfish. Clownfish live among the stinging arms of big **anemones** (say *an-em-o-nees*). Clownfish have special slime on their skin that stops the anemones from stinging them.

This is the eye of the stonefish. These creatures are very hard to see around rocks.

I always look out for stonefish. The stonefish is one of the hardest sea creatures to find. This fish, which looks exactly like a rock, waits for smaller fish to swim past, then leaps up and swallows them whole.

Many animals live on the Great Barrier Reef. There are corals, seastars, clams, shrimps and sea slugs. These creatures are different from fish because they have no backbone. They are called **invertebrates** (say *in-ver-ti-bruts*).

This little sea slug has bright colours to let fish know it is poisonous to eat.

Chapter Three

Snorkelling

Scuba diving is not the only way that I can see the underwater world. Sometimes, I leave my heavy tank behind and go snorkelling. It's great not having to carry all that weight!

When I see something interesting, I fill my lungs with air then dive down for a closer look. I can hold my breath long enough to dive down more than 20 metres.

This photo shows me surrounded by a whirlpool of big silver fish.

I have seen large schools of Barracouta fish. These fish reach one metre in length and have razor-sharp teeth. Barracoutas hunt other fish.

Sometimes, when I go out into the blue water away from the reef, green turtles swim past me. These big turtles travel the oceans eating jellyfish. They lay their eggs on sand islands along the Great Barrier Reef.

Chapter Four

Night Diving

It's very exciting to go diving at night.
I use a large waterproof torch so I can see
where I'm going. Night diving can be a bit
scary, but the awesome creatures I see soon
make me forget to be afraid.

moray eel

I see very different creatures when I dive at night. **Nocturnal** creatures, such as this moray eel, come out at night to hunt for sleeping fish.

Other nocturnal creatures use the cover of darkness to hide from big fish such as sharks and Barracouta.

This parrotfish is asleep. Fish don't have eyelids so they sleep with their eyes open. Scientists don't know if sleeping fish dream.

16

During one night dive, I found a cuttlefish. Cuttlefish are experts at changing the colour and shape of their skin. They can make their skin spiky or smooth and dark or light. Cuttlefish can even have one side of their body showing one pattern while the other side shows another.

This is a special sort of lobster, called a Slipper Lobster. It digs in the sand for its food.

Lobsters also come out at night to feed. They walk around hunting for shells and spiny sea urchins. During the day, lobsters hide deep in caves or under the sand, away from sharks who love to eat them.

Another night-time creature is the Blue-spotted Stingray. It comes out of hiding to feed. The stingray has special sensors in its skin. The sensors detect the weak electricity that is given off by some animals buried under the sand. This is how they find and dig up their food.

This is a baby shrimp about the size of a jelly bean.

Many tiny creatures float around in the water. They are invisible during the day because they are see-through. Light from a torch helps us see them under the water. These animals are called plankton.

Chapter Five

Shark Dive

The best place to dive is at Osprey Reef.
This is a great place to see my favourite
animals — sharks. It is also popular with
film-makers. They come from all around the
world to film sharks at this reef.

I always go to a special rock where the sharks come in close. Some get close enough to touch.

Different types of sharks come here. These ones are White-tip Reef Sharks. Their name comes from the white tips on the ends of their fins. They usually swim near the sea floor.

Occasionally, I see more than 50 sharks in a single dive. This is a Grey Reef Shark. They are not as friendly as White-tip Reef Sharks, and they are much faster swimmers.

Hammerhead sharks also visit here. They have rectangular heads with nostrils on each end. The shape of their head helps them to search for food. If the smell is stronger in one nostril, they steer that way until they find their prey.

Sharks aren't the only creatures of Osprey Reef. Big Potato Cods also live there. They are not afraid of people. Potato Cods will come up very close to see if a diver has anything to eat.

I'm always excited when I'm on a diving expedition. I never know what the next day will bring. The seas are full of amazing creatures and every dive brings new surprises. I love living on the Great Barrier Reef.

Glossary

anemones (say *an-em-o-nees*) ocean animals with stinging arms.

compressed forced into a small space.

expeditions trips for a special purpose.

invertebrates (say *in-ver-ti-bruts*) animals with no backbone.

marine having to do with the sea.

nocturnal active at night.

reef a ridge of rock or coral near the surface of the sea.

scuba special equipment that lets a diver breathe air from a tank.

Index